Contents

Any words appearing in the text in bold, **like this**, are explained in the glossary.

日本山妙法寺
献燈
富士道場

REGIONS OF THE WORLD

North and East Asia

Neil Morris

www.heinemann.co.uk/library
Visit our website to find out more information about Heinemann Library books.

To order:
Phone 44 (0) 1865 888112

Send a fax to 44 (0) 1865 314091
Visit the Heinemann bookshop at www.heinemann.co.uk/library to browse our catalogue and order online.

First published in Great Britain by Heinemann Library, Halley Court, Jordan Hill, Oxford OX2 8EJ, part of Harcourt Education.
Heinemann is a registered trademark of Harcourt Education Ltd.

First published in paperback 2009

Editorial: Andrew Farrow
Design: Steve Mead and Q2A Creative
Illustrations: International Mapping Associates, Inc
Picture Research: Melissa Allison
Production: Alison Parsons

Originated by Chroma Graphics (Overseas) Pte.
Printed and bound in China by Leo Paper Group

ISBN 978 0 431 90714 7 (hardback)

12 11 10 09 08
10 9 8 7 6 5 4 3 2 1

ISBN 978 0 431 90723 9 (paperback)

13 12 11 10 9
10 9 8 7 6 5 4 3 2 1

British Library Cataloguing in Publication Data
Morris, Neil, 1946-
North and East Asia. - (Regions of the world)
1. Asia - Geography - Juvenile literature
I. Title
915

A full catalogue record for this book is available fro
the British Library.

Acknowledgements
The publishers would like to thank the following for permission to reproduce photographs:

© Alamy pp. **25** (Arco Images), **51** (Images&Stories), **31** (Mediacolor's), **8** (Robert Harding World Imagery), **18** (Worldwide Picture Library); © ChinaStock p. **22** (Dennis Cox); © Corbis pp. **29, 42** (Michel Setboun), **52** (Corbis Royalty-free), **39** (Alain Nogues), **17** (Dean Conger), **36** (Catherine Karnow), **54** (epa/Wu Hong), **26** (Jose Fuste Raga), **10** (Kazuyoshi Nomachi), **28** (Ramin Talaie), **41** (Richard T. Nowitz), **49** (Zack Seckler); © PA Photos pp. **27, 40** (AP), **34** (AP/Shizuo Kambayashi), **44** (AP/Xinhua, Du Huaju); © OSF p. **13** (Konrad Wothe); © Robert Harding pp. **47** (Bruno Morandi), **38** (David Beatty), **14** (Gavin Hellier), **33** (Gina Corrigan), **16** (PanoramaStock); © Photoshot p. **4** (World Pictures).

Cover photograph of a Khampa girl at a monastery in the Tibetan kingdom of Kham reproduced with permission of OnAsia Images/Leisa Tyler.

The publishers would like to thank Daniel Block for his assistance in the preparation of this book.

Introducing North and East Asia

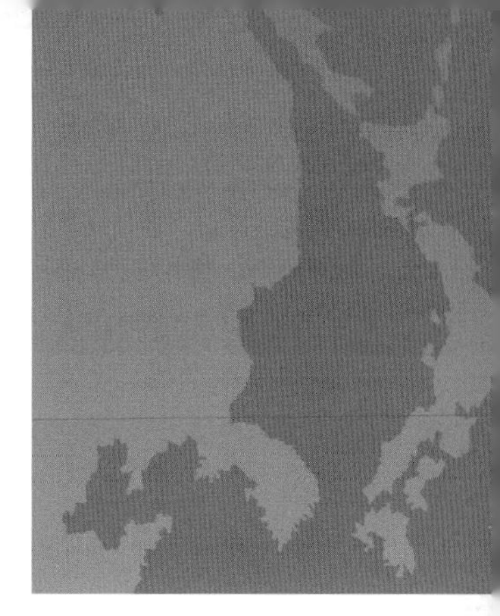

The vast region of North and East Asia covers nearly two-thirds of the world's largest **continent**. To the west, the Ural Mountains form a natural boundary between Asia and Europe. Together, the two continents make up an even bigger landmass that geographers call Eurasia. The Urals divide the world's largest country, Russia, which covers the entire area of northern Asia. The mountains stretch south to Kazakhstan, the largest of the five countries that make up Central Asia.

The eastern part of this Asian region is dominated by China, the world's third largest country in area and its largest in terms of population. The first unified Chinese empire was formed more than 2,000 years ago, and China has played a vital role in world development ever since. Over the years its civilization greatly influenced neighbouring Korea, which is now divided into two countries, and the islands of Japan. South of the region covered by this book lie the mainland and islands of Southeast Asia, and the Asian subcontinent of India.

← Japanese children enjoy an outing. In the background is the beautiful snow-capped peak of Mount Fuji.

Largest countries

Four of the region's twelve countries are much larger than the others. Three of them are in the world's top ten in terms of area – Russia (1st), China (3rd, after Canada) and Kazakhstan (9th). Together with Mongolia, these countries make up more than 90 percent of the region's area. The four countries also form borders with each other.

The Asian part of Russia, which is also called Siberia, is three times bigger than the European part and would be the largest country in the world on its own (without the European territory). If you travelled from the industrial city of Magnitogorsk, on the Asian side of the Ural Mountains, to the town of Egvekinot, on the Bering Sea coast in northeast Russia, you would cover more than 5,800 kilometres (3,600 miles). You would also cross seven **time zones**.

China and Mongolia

Modern China is six times bigger than its northern neighbour, Mongolia. The Mongols were an Asian people who built a vast empire during the 13th century, by conquering an area from their homeland to western Asia and eastern Europe. The Mongol leader Kublai Khan founded the Yuan **dynasty** that ruled the Chinese empire from 1279 to 1368. The Mongol empire then broke up towards the end of the 14th century.

China ruled Mongolia as part of its empire from 1691 to 1911, when the territory was called Outer Mongolia. This was to distinguish it from Inner Mongolia (or Neimenggu), which is still an **autonomous** region of the People's Republic of China and is three-quarters the size of the present independent state of Mongolia. While the population of Mongolia is mainly descended from the Mongols, a large majority of the people of Inner Mongolia are Han Chinese (see page 23). Overall, less than a fifth of the Chinese territory's people are of Mongol descent.

SMALLEST COUNTRY

The region's smallest country is the island of Taiwan, which lies in the South China Sea off the Chinese mainland. It is less than half the size of the next smallest country, South Korea. But is Taiwan really a country at all? Though the Taiwanese call their state the Republic of China (ROC), the People's Republic of China claims it as part of its territory (see page 28).

This political map shows the 12 independent countries of the region covered in this book. All the countries and their statistics are listed on page 56.

East Asian civilization

The Chinese civilization is one of the oldest in the world. People were living in East Asia long before the beginning of written history. Ancestors of the Chinese people formed farming settlements along the valleys of two great rivers – the Huang He (or Yellow River) and the Chang Jiang (or Yangtze) – about 9,000 years ago. Near the more northerly Huang He, farming families grew millet, as well as hunting game and fishing in the river. The Huang He is the world's muddiest river, and it was named after its muddy yellow colour. Further south, people built houses on stilts on the marshy land next to the Chang Jiang, or "long river". They used the flooded marshes to grow rice.

The Huang He river carries a great deal of **silt**. This is a fine layer of mud and clay. It makes the nearby soil especially fertile.

The first Chinese dynasty to leave a historical record was the Shang dynasty. The beginning of their rule is usually dated at 1766 BCE. The ancient people of the Korean **peninsula** were greatly influenced by the powerful Chinese empire. In 108 BCE the Korean empire of Choson was taken over by warriors of the Han dynasty that then ruled China. The islands of Japan were similarly influenced. In CE 57, Japanese messengers travelled to China, and over the next few hundred years many new ideas crossed the sea back to Japan. The Japanese borrowed the Chinese system of writing, which used symbols, and adapted it to suit their own spoken language. They also learned many arts and crafts from China: how to cast bronze, make fine **porcelain**, and weave silk. In 552, Buddhism came to Japan from China and Korea.

Former Soviet Union

The five countries of Central Asia are linked by more recent history. Kazakhstan, Kyrgyzstan, Tajikistan, Turkmenistan, and Uzbekistan were, along with Russia, former republics of the Soviet Union (or USSR, the

Union of Soviet Socialist Republics). This communist state came into being in 1922 and broke up in 1991. The former republics then gained their independence. The largest Central Asian country, Kazakhstan, is more than five times bigger than the next biggest, Turkmenistan.

The ruling dynasties of China

Date	Dynasty	Date	Dynasty
1766–1045 BCE	Shang	618–907	Tang
1045–256 BCE	Zhou	960–1279	Song
221–206 BCE	Qin	1368–1644	Ming
206 BCE–220 CE	Han	1644–1912	Qing
581–618	Sui		

COMMONWEALTH OF INDEPENDENT STATES

Four of the five Central Asian countries are members of the Commonwealth of Independent States (CIS), which has its headquarters in Minsk, Belarus. This is a loose association of many of the former Soviet republics, that was created to help them work together, especially economically. The odd one out is Turkmenistan, which reduced its role in the CIS to that of associate member in 2005. The Turkmen government said they did this because they wanted to remain neutral (and not favour any side in a dispute or conflict). Turkmenistan has never signed the CIS Security Treaty, which today has seven member countries.

Though this and many other agreements have been signed between the different members since 1991, the CIS has no formal **charter**. Member countries are working towards creating a free trade zone, similar to the European Union, so that they can trade with each other without paying taxes. As by far the largest member, Russia has great influence in the CIS. It would like Russian to be an official language throughout the CIS. So far only Kyrgyzstan has accepted this.

Natural features

Asia is bounded by the cold Arctic Ocean to the north and the much warmer Pacific Ocean to the east. Both oceans have long Asian coastlines, and Japan and Taiwan are islands in the Pacific. Asia's western boundary with Europe is formed by the Ural Mountains. Continuing south, the area of Central Asia borders the Caspian Sea and the countries of Iran and Afghanistan. The high mountain peaks of the Himalayas make a natural boundary between China and the countries of southern Asia – India and the smaller kingdoms of Nepal and Bhutan.

The Russian region of Siberia, with its **tundra** and **taiga** (see page 13), makes up North Asia. Siberia can be divided into three, with a plain to the west, a central **plateau** between the Yenisei and Lena rivers, and uplands to the east with a series of mountain ranges. Central Asia has rocky plateaus and deserts that stretch into Mongolia and China. East Asia includes the highlands of the Tibetan Plateau, the fertile farming regions of China, and the mountains, hills, and volcanoes of Japan.

← These boats were left stranded by the shrinking of the Aral Sea (see page 19). They have quickly rusted from the huge amounts of dust and salt.

Coastlines

The coastline of northern Siberia (Asian Russia) lies entirely above the Arctic Circle, so it is very cold indeed. Many parts have an average air temperature of 2 °C (35.6 °F) in mid-summer and –30 °C (–22 °F) in mid-winter. The coast is covered with ice for most of the year, and most parts are navigable only in August and September.

Along the Pacific coastline of North and East Asia, the ocean is divided into six sections: the Bering, Okhotsk, Japan, Yellow, East China, and South China Seas. The Siberian coastline along the Bering and Okhotsk Seas, which are divided by the Kamchatka Peninsula (see page 15), is cold. Some parts are covered with ice for at least seven months of the year. Further south, the **climate** is quite different. The island of Hainan, in the tropical South China Sea, is very warm in summer and mild in winter.

Tundra and taiga

Northern Siberia is made up of tundra, a treeless plain where the subsoil is permanently frozen. This is called **permafrost**. Water cannot drain away, so in summer the tundra becomes marshy. To the south of this cold region lies a vast **coniferous** forest called taiga, full of cedar, fir, pine, and spruce trees. This vast forest continues into northern Europe and North America, and is the biggest forest in the world.

Largest island

Japan is made up of four main islands and thousands of smaller ones. The largest Japanese island – Honshu – makes up well over half of the country's land area. Like other Japanese islands, Honshu has many volcanoes and suffers from earthquakes. This is because the islands are situated where four separate pieces of the Earth's crust meet. When the pieces, called plates, move or crack along fault lines, the Earth shakes.

BERING STRAIT

A narrow **strait** connects the Chukchi and Bering Seas, separating the **continents** of Asia and North America. It is named after the Danish sailor Vitus Bering (1681–1741), who went in search of a land bridge between the two continents. The strait is 85 kilometres (53 miles) wide and up to 52 metres (171 feet) deep. It is covered in ice for much of the year. During the last Ice Age the sea level fell, leaving a land bridge between the two continents. Some time between 20,000 and 15,000 years ago, **nomadic** hunter-gatherers crossed from Asia – the first humans to set foot in the Americas.

Rivers flow northwards through the taiga to the Arctic Ocean (see page 17). Some streams form lakes in the forest.

Japan's highest peak is famous Mount Fuji (3,776 metres/12,389 feet). It has been dormant since 1707, but is still classified as an active volcano. Further inland lies Mount Asama (2,568 metres/8,425 feet), a truly active volcano that last erupted in 2004. Since 1988, Honshu has been linked to Japan's next largest island, Hokkaido, by the world's longest tunnel. The Seikan rail tunnel is nearly 54 kilometres (34 miles) long.

This physical map shows the topography of the region.

These are the peaks of the Tian Shan range, seen from a valley in Kyrgyzstan.

Mountain ranges

The Himalayas lie between the Plateau of Tibet and the Indian **subcontinent**. This is the world's highest mountain range, and it includes nine of the ten highest peaks on Earth. Many of these are on the Chinese border, including the highest peak of all, Mount Everest. Known to the people of Tibet as Qomolangma, or "Goddess mother of the world", this famous mountain reaches 8,850 metres (29,035 feet) above sea level. The Himalayan peaks are all above the snow line, which begins at about 4,500 metres (14,760 feet) and is about 1000 metres (3,280 feet) above the tree line.

The range of the Tian Shan (Chinese for "heavenly mountains") forms a natural border between Kyrgyzstan and the neighbouring Xinjiang province of China. The range is about 2,400 kilometres (1,500 miles) long (compared with 3,800 kilometres/2,360 miles for the Himalayas) and is full of snow-capped peaks, **glaciers**, and deep **gorges**. The highest mountain is Pik Pobedy (Russian for "Victory Peak"), which rises to 7,439 metres (24,406 feet) on the Kyrgyzstan–China border.

Roof of the World

The Plateau of Tibet is often called the Roof of the World. The world's highest plateau has an average altitude of more than 4,800 metres (15,700 feet), and is bounded by the Kunlun Mountains to the north and the Himalayas to the south. In an area larger than Mongolia, it contains the **headwaters** of many long rivers, including the Brahmaputra, Chang Jiang, Huang He, Indus, and Mekong.

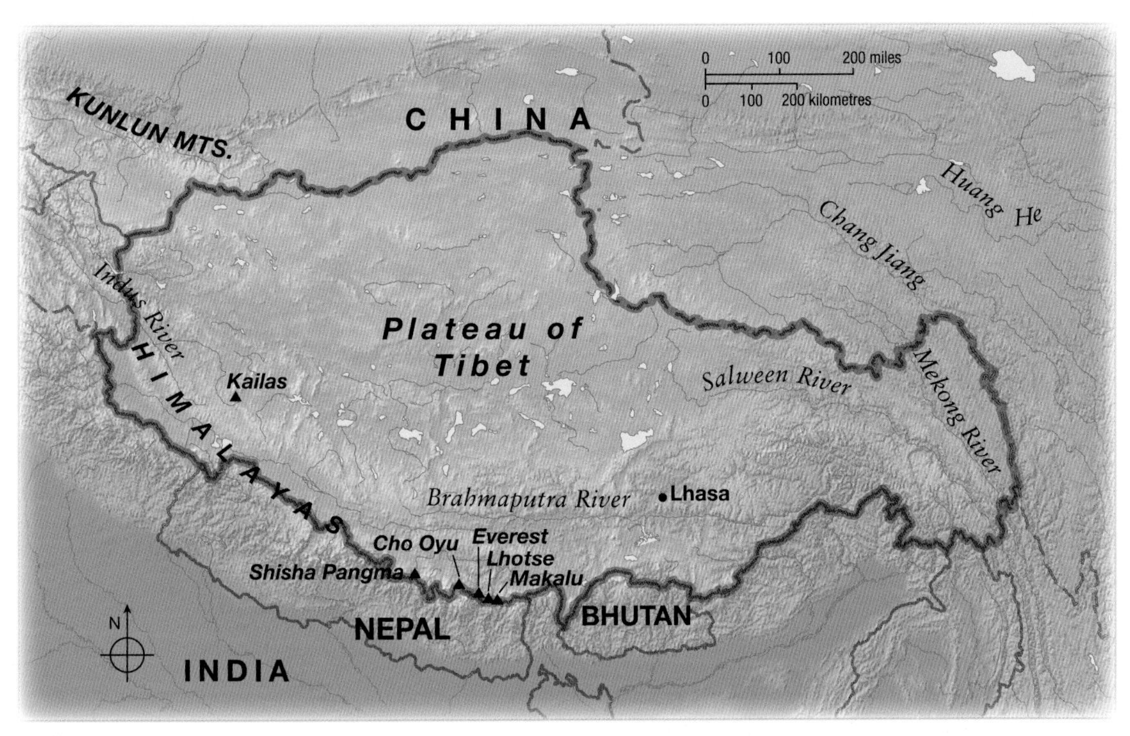

The red outline shows the borders of the Chinese autonomous region of Tibet (see page 31). The Plateau of Tibet is dotted with lakes. There are many high peaks on its border with Nepal, including Mount Everest.

MOUNT KAILAS

This Himalayan peak lies to the southwest of the Tibetan Plateau and rises to 6,714 metres (22,028 feet). It is a perfect peak, shaped like a pyramid or four-sided crystal. Perhaps that is why, although remote, it attracts Hindu and Buddhist **pilgrims**. To Hindus it represents the paradise of the supreme god Shiva. Tibetan Buddhists believe Kailas to be Mount Sumeru, the very centre of their universe. Pilgrims do not climb the sacred mountain, but walk around its base. The pilgrim path stretches for more than 50 kilometres (30 miles).

Volcanic peninsula

Russia's Kamchatka Peninsula is about 1200 kilometres (745 miles) long and up to 480 kilometres (298 miles) across. Two mountain ranges run down the peninsula, and they contain more than 300 volcanoes, at least 29 of which are active. The highest volcanic peak is Klyuchevskoy (4,750 metres/15,584 feet), which last erupted in 2005. The peninsula forms a small part of the volcanic **Ring of Fire** that circles the Pacific Ocean.

Riverboats pass through the Qutang Gorge (one of the famous Three Gorges) on the Chang Jiang.

From plateau to ocean

Asia's longest and third longest rivers flow for thousands of kilometres eastwards from the Plateau of Tibet to the Pacific Ocean. The Chang Jiang (sometimes called the Yangtze River) rises on the plateau at a height of 4,880 metres (16,011 feet) and is joined by more than 700 **tributaries** on its way to the ocean. This enormous river (at 6,300 kilometres/3,916 miles the third longest in the world, after the Nile and the Amazon) drains more than 1.8 million square kilometres (695,000 square miles) of land – nearly a fifth of the whole area of China. In its upper reaches the river passes through steep, narrow gorges, and in places the Chinese have built dams to turn the river's power into hydroelectricity. A vast new **hydroelectric** project, the Three Gorges Dam (see page 45), will soon be completed.

The Huang He (or Yellow River, 5,464 kilometres/3,396 miles long) is more useful for agriculture. It is an unpredictable river, however, since in many places its banks are low. It fertilizes the land with its rich silt, but it is also prone to floods. It has changed its course many times, and at different times has poured into the Yellow Sea at points as much as 800 kilometres (500 miles) apart.

About 2,500 years ago, the Chinese began building a canal that today connects the Chang Jiang and the Huang He. The Grand Canal is more than 1,700 kilometres (1,050 miles) long, connecting the northern capital city of Beijing with Hangzhou in the south.

To the Arctic

Several vast rivers flow northwards through Siberia to the Arctic Ocean. The longest, the Yenisei (5,540 kilometres/3,443 miles), begins as the River Selenga, which flows into Lake Baikal. This river's vast drainage basin covers more than one fifth of Siberia. The Yenisei flows across the western section of the Central Siberian Plateau, and as it nears the ocean it starts to freeze over in October each year. It remains frozen until May or June.

The Ob (5,410 kilometres/3,362 miles) is the second longest Siberian river, when measured from the source of its biggest **tributary**, the Irtysh. This river also freezes each winter, when its 725 kilometre-long (450 mile-long) estuary is blocked with ice.

LAKE BAIKAL

A total of 336 rivers flow into the deepest lake in the world, in southeastern Russia. Yet Lake Baikal has just one outlet, River Angara, a tributary of the Yenisei. **Geologists** think the lake was formed about 25 million years ago by movements in the Earth's crust. Its surface usually freezes from January to May. In recent years, industry on its shores has caused pollution. The area has now become a national park, and **environmentalists** are working to protect it.

Lake Baikal plunges down to 1,620 metres (5,315 feet). It is estimated that the lake contains more than one fifth of the world's unfrozen fresh water.

The rugged terrain of the Karakum. This dry region beside the Amu Darya River has long, hot summers and very mild winters, with average annual rainfall of less than 150 millimetres (5.9 inches).

Biggest deserts

The region's largest desert, the Gobi, stretches for about 1.3 million square kilometres (502,000 square miles) across the borders of Mongolia and China. It lies on a plateau, between 900 metres (2,950 feet) and 1,500 metres (4,900 feet) high, and its position means that the desert has extreme weather. In summer there are long heatwaves, when the temperature can rise to 45 °C (113 °F). In winter, however, the temperature can drop to –40 °C (–40 °F), and spring and autumn are also cold. A desert is usually defined as a region that receives less than 250 millimetres (10 inches) of rain a year. The western part of the Gobi gets 69 millimetres (2.7 inches), and the northeast 200 millimetres (7.9 inches).

China's Takla Makan desert lies to the west of the Gobi, and is about a quarter of its size. It is surrounded on three sides by mountain ranges – the Tian Shan (see page 14), the Pamir and the Kunlun mountains. The desert's **precipitation** is less than 40 millimetres (1.6 inches) per year. To the east of the desert is a great bowl of dry rock, called the Turfan Depression, which lies at 154 metres (505 feet) below sea level.

Black and Red Sands

There are two large deserts in Central Asia – the Karakum (meaning "black sands") in Turkmenistan, and the Kyzylkum (meaning "red sands") in Kazakhstan and Uzbekistan. To the south of the Karakum desert, a canal from the Amu Darya River **irrigates** the land for growing cotton, fruits, and cereals. This irrigation has caused problems in other areas, such as the Aral Sea. The Kyzylkum lies between the Syr Darya and Amu Darya rivers, to the southeast of the Aral Sea.

Deserts of the region

Desert	Countries
Gobi	China, Mongolia
Takla Makan	China
Karakum	Turkmenistan
Kyzylkum	Kazakhstan, Uzbekistan

GROWING DESERTS

Many parts of Central Asia face the problem of desertification – the process by which dry regions grow bigger, spread, and become deserts. A special case is the Aral Sea, which lies between Uzbekistan and Kazakhstan. In 1960, this was the fourth largest lake in the world, covering an area of about 68,000 square kilometres (26,300 square miles). Now it is little more than 17,000 square kilometres (6,500 square miles) and has dropped to number 16 in the world list, behind Lake Balkhash in southeastern Kazakhstan.

The lake's water comes from two rivers, the Amu Darya and Syr Darya, both of which have been diverted to provide irrigation for cotton farming in Turkmenistan and elsewhere. The Aral Sea has no outlets and is a salt lake. With little water now reaching it, fishing villages that were on the shoreline 30 years ago are now many kilometres from the lake. The uncovered land has dried up, leaving behind huge amounts of salt (see photo, page 10).

Climate

This region includes latitudes from above the Arctic Circle, in northern Siberia, to just below the Tropic of Cancer in southeast China. **Climate** is very different at these two latitudes. The Arctic region is freezing in winter and cool in summer, and the land is covered for much of the year by snow and ice. Siberia has the most extreme climate in the world. In Verkhoyansk, just above the Arctic Circle to the east of the River Lena, a near record low of –66.7 °C (–88.1 °F) was recorded in January 2006. As the table opposite shows, this Siberian town records much less than the 250 millimetres (10 inches) of precipitation that is the limit for a desert. That is why geographers consider much of the Arctic region to be a cold desert.

In complete contrast to Siberia, near the coast of the warm South China Sea the climate is warm all year round. In Hong Kong, the average winter temperature is higher than that for summer in Siberia. But the amount of precipitation (mostly snow in Siberia, rain in Hong Kong) is very different too – there is more than 16 times as much in the tropical south. In the figures opposite, those for Ulan Bator and Qazaly reflect the climates of the Mongolian and Kazakh desert regions.

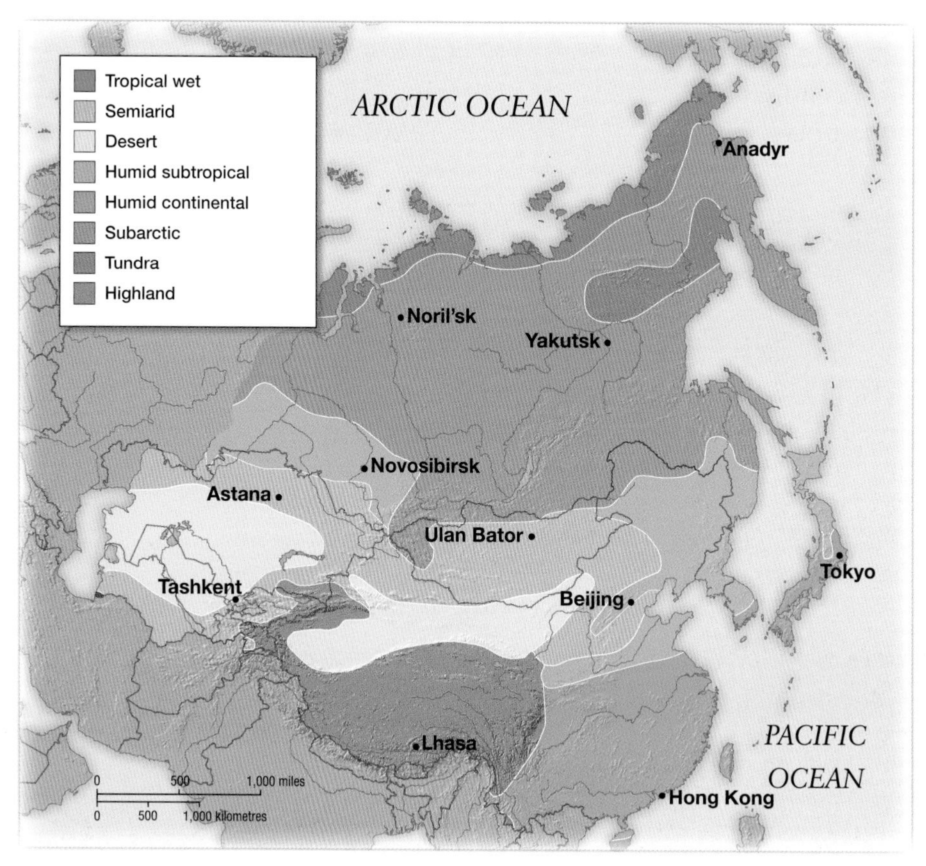

This map shows the **subarctic** climate of much of North Asia, the arid climate of Central Asia, and the generally temperate climate of East Asia.

Latitude, temperature, and precipitation

	Latitude ° north	Average annual temp °C (°F)	Jan temp °C (°F)	July temp °C (°F)	Precipitation in mm (in.)
Verkhoyansk, Russia	67°33′	–17 (1.4)	–50 (–58)	14 (57.2)	134 (5.3)
Ulan Bator, Mongolia	47°54′	–3 (26.6)	–26 (–14.8)	16 (60.8)	208 (8.2)
Qazaly, Kazakhstan	45°46′	7 (44.6)	–12 (10.4)	23 (73.4)	125 (4.9)
Tokyo, Japan	35°40′	14 (57.2)	3 (37.4)	25 (77)	1,565 (61.6)
Hong Kong, China	22°17′	23 (73.4)	16 (60.8)	28 (82.4)	2,162 (85.1)

Seasonal winds

Seasonal winds called **monsoons** greatly affect the region's climate. In winter, winds from the north and west of the region blow into East Asia and cause cold, dry weather and sometimes dust storms. In summer, the wind switches direction and blows from the Pacific Ocean and spreads warm, moist air. This means that most of East Asia's rain falls between May and October. If the summer monsoon is strong, it may carry rain all the way to Mongolia. But a weak monsoon year can lead to crop failure in southern China.

TYPHOONS

Along the Pacific coast of Asia, tropical storms are called **typhoons** (from the Chinese *tai fung*, meaning "big wind"). These devastating storms usually occur between June and November, and many pass through the South China Sea. In August 2006, China was hit by its eighth storm of the year and the strongest for half a century. Typhoon Saomai, with winds of more than 200 kph (124 mph), moved in off the Pacific, bringing heavy rainfall to Taiwan and causing 1.5 million people on the Chinese mainland to be evacuated from their homes.

Tropical cyclones (or typhoons) form over warm oceans with a water temperature of at least 27 °C (80.6 °F). The world's oceans are generally getting warmer, and many experts believe that this is due to **global warming**, caused by an increase in our production of **greenhouse gases**. In turn, this may cause more hurricanes and typhoons. Between 1975 and 1989 there was an average of five severe typhoons each year in the northwest Pacific region. From 1990 to 2004 this yearly average figure increased to nearly eight.

People

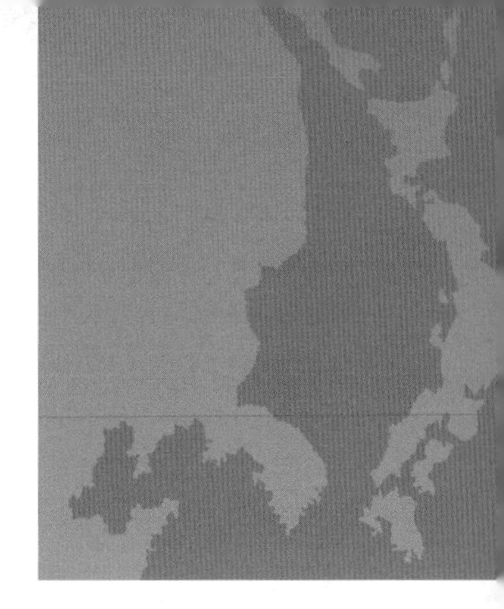

Asia is the world's largest **continent** in terms of population. Taken together, the north, east, and central areas of Asia account for 42 percent of the continent's people. China has the largest population of any country in the world, with more than 1.3 billion people. In the region, the next largest populations live in Japan (with 128 million people), South Korea (48 million) and Asian Russia (37 million).

There are many different ethnic groups in the region, each with its own language, culture, and traditions. The greatest number live in the most populous country, China, where the government officially recognizes more than 50 different ethnic groups. Han Chinese represent the largest number, and make up more than 90 percent of the total population. This makes the Han the world's largest ethnic group, but still there are great cultural differences within the group. In some other, smaller countries, cultural differences have arisen in recent times. Since Korea was divided in 1948, the people of the two countries (North and South) have come to live different lives. Yet they are all descended from the same ethnic group, and they speak the same language, Korean.

← A crowd of cyclists in China's capital, Beijing. This large city's population is continuing to expand (see page 27).

Where people live

The region's total population of more than 1.6 billion people is distributed very unevenly across the 12 countries. The region's overall average **population density** – that is, the number of people who live in one square kilometre – is 58 (150 per square mile). The rest of the Asian continent is generally more populated, bringing the continent's average up to 90 people per square kilometre (233 per square mile).

Population density

Area	People per sq km (sq mile)	Area	People per sq km (sq mile)
Region	58 (150)	Tajikistan	46 (119)
Taiwan	632 (1,637)	Kyrgyzstan	27 (70)
South Korea	487 (1,261)	Turkmenistan	10 (26)
Japan	339 (878)	Kazakhstan	6 (16)
North Korea	190 (492)	(Asian) Russia	3 (8)
China	140 (363)	Mongolia	2 (5)
Uzbekistan	61 (158)		

As the table above shows, much of the region is far less densely populated than the average. Many of the northern areas are so cold, and other areas so dry or mountainous, that few people live there. Kazakhstan has just 6 people per square kilometre (16 per square mile), while Asian Russia has half that number and Mongolia has just 2 people per square kilometre (5 per square mile).

The smallest country in the region, Taiwan, has the highest population density (more than 10 times the regional average). The most populous country, China, is so large that its density works out at 140 per square kilometre (363 per square mile).

Chinese growth

China's huge population has been growing steadily in recent years. It was 1 billion people in 1981, and is now 1.3 billion. United Nations forecasters say this may increase to 1.4 billion by 2010 and 1.5 billion by 2025. As in many other parts of the world, the average age of the population is changing, too. Today about a third of the Chinese population is under 19 years old, and less than a quarter is over 50. It is estimated that by 2025 the young age group may have shrunk to less than a quarter, and the older group to more than a third. This will mean that the younger, working population will have a lot more older, retired people to look after.

This Chinese poster aims to promote the idea of the one-child family as ideal. Many people disagree with this idea and its enforcement as a national policy.

PLANNED BIRTH POLICY

In 1979, when the country's population was 975 million, the Chinese government introduced a policy to limit population growth. Couples were encouraged to have only one child, and in some towns and cities this was a strict requirement. Regulations have changed since then, and they vary from place to place within the country. In many rural areas, families are allowed to have a second child if the first child is a girl and is at least three years old. Couples who break the rules face fines and penalties.

The Chinese authorities say that these policies have had great benefits, and it has been estimated that the population would be 300 million higher without them. But many people feel that the idea of a state controlling the size of families is a violation of basic human rights.

The city of Seoul was founded in 1394. Some of the ancient gates into the city have been restored and still stand. As in other modern cities, many of Seoul's new buildings are skyscrapers.

Urban trends

In recent years, people globally have been moving from the countryside (rural areas) to towns and cities (urban areas). The United Nations forecasts that in the near future the global urban–rural split will be 50–50. In Asia, the urban population has grown by nearly a third over the past 10 years, but the urban percentage is still less than the world average. As the chart below shows, the urban population in North, East, and Central Asia still counts for less than half the people. But in many countries, including South Korea and Japan, the urban figure is much higher.

Biggest cities

Two of the region's most populous cities are in Japan, including the world's largest city – Tokyo. Another is Seoul, in South Korea. In China, 35 cities have more than a million people. Shenzhen, near Hong Kong, was a small town of just 20,000 people when the Chinese government made it a Special Economic Zone in 1979 and developed it for business and industry. People moved there from all over the country, and it now has a population of more than 7 million people.

Urban-rural population

Area	Urban–rural population %
World	48–52
Region	44–56
South Korea	81–19
Taiwan	78–22
(Asian) Russia	70–30
Japan	66–34
North Korea	62–38
Kazakhstan	57–43
Mongolia	57–43
Turkmenistan	46–54
China	40–60
Uzbekistan	37–63
Kyrgyzstan	36–64
Tajikistan	25–75

The Taipei 101 building, in Taiwan's capital city, Taipei, is the world's tallest building. Completed in 2004, it has 101 floors and is 508 metres (1,667 feet) high. The building has 61 lifts to service shops, offices, restaurants, and observation decks.

Population of cities

City	2005 population in millions	2015 estimated population in millions	City	2005 population in millions	2015 estimated population in millions
Tokyo, Japan	35.1	35.4	Guangzhou, China	8.4	10.4
Shanghai, China	14.5	17.2	Shenzhen, China	7.2	8.9
Osaka-Kobe, Japan	11.2	11.3	Hong Kong, China	7.0	7.7
Beijing, China	10.7	12.8	Tianjin, China	7.0	8.1
Seoul, South Korea	9.6	9.5	Chonqing, China	6.3	7.2

DEVELOPING BEIJING FOR 2008

Beijing is an ancient city, first founded as a trading centre about 4,000 years ago. When it was chosen to host the 2008 Olympic Games, the Chinese authorities began a complete redevelopment of their capital city. Old narrow roads and alleys have been demolished to make way for wider streets. An urban motorway and two ring roads around the city are being built. There is a new railway line from the airport, which will soon have the world's largest terminal. In 2006, all the work was on schedule, including the new Olympic stadium.

The Chinese delegate at the United Nations is from the People's Republic of China. The Taiwanese have no representative there.

Communist states

Communism is a political system based on the communal ownership of property and wealth, with regulated markets. Unlike the other countries of the region, which vary in their forms of democratic government, China and North Korea are communist states. But the two countries are very different from each other. China is still dominated by the Communist Party, but in recent years the authorities have stopped regulating the economy so strongly. Private business owners are now encouraged, and since 2002 they have even been allowed to join the Communist Party. The Chinese economy is now growing extremely fast (see page 43), with more private enterprise and fewer state-run industries.

In North Korea, the communist organization of the Korean Workers' Party holds complete power. North Korea is one of the world's most secretive states, so we do not know what life there is like for ordinary people. We do know that televisions and radios are pre-tuned to government stations, so people only see and hear what their leaders want them to. According to the media rights organization Reporters Without Borders, North Korea is the world's worst violator of press freedom: "The entire North Korean press is under the direct control of Kim Jong-il [General Secretary of the Korean Workers' Party]."

PRC and ROC

The official title of China is the People's Republic of China (PRC). The small island country of Taiwan is officially called the Republic of China (ROC). The split between the two Chinas came about in 1949, when Nationalists opposed to communism were defeated by communist forces on the mainland. The non-communists fled to the island that was then called Formosa (now Taiwan). At first, the United Nations recognized and supported Taiwan, rather than the People's Republic of China. But in 1971 they decided that the PRC should represent China at the UN instead. Today, the dispute between the two Chinas has still not been resolved. Most of the world's nations officially accept that Taiwan is a province of the PRC. Because of this, the ROC has formal diplomatic relations with only 24 countries around the world.

North and South Korea

Communist North Korea is officially the Democratic People's Republic of Korea (Korean name Choson), while South Korea is the Republic of Korea (Korean name Han Kook). For the first half of the 20th century, Korea was under Japanese rule, but after World War II (1939–45) the Allies decided to divide the country. When the north invaded the south in 1950, the Korean War broke out. The north was backed by China and the Soviet Union, the south was backed by the USA and other countries in the United Nations. The war lasted until 1953, without victory to either side. It also ended without a formal peace agreement, and there remains constant tension between the two Koreas.

DEMILITARIZED ZONE

The border between North and South Korea is formed by a Demilitarized Zone (or DMZ). This neutral zone is 248 kilometres (154 miles) long and about 4 kilometres (2.5 miles) wide, and it is there to act as a buffer between the two states. It is known as the last frontier of the **Cold War** between communists and **capitalists**, which used to exist between the Soviet Union on one side, and the USA and their allies on the other. The DMZ is known as the world's most heavily fortified frontier.

These North Korean soldiers are patrolling the border with South Korea in the Demilitarized Zone.

Religions

Many different religions are represented in the region. In Russia, the major religion is Christianity, and about one fifth of the population belong to the Russian Orthodox Church. This form of Christianity dates from the 10th century and was historically associated with the Russian Empire, but it was discouraged during the rule of the Soviet Union. There are small Christian minorities in many other of the region's countries.

The Chinese government does not encourage religious practice, but some people follow the traditional philosophies of Confucianism and Taoism, as well as Buddhism. Confucian philosophy and Buddhism are also popular in South Korea, and more than a quarter of South Koreans are Christians. Buddhism is also followed in Taiwan. About half the people of Mongolia follow Lamaism, a form of Buddhism that is also practised in Tibet (see opposite). In Japan, most people follow practices or rituals based on Buddhism and an ancient Japanese religion called Shinto (meaning "way of the gods"). Strict Shintoists worship and make offerings to gods and spirits associated with the natural world.

Islam is the biggest religion in the countries of Central Asia, but forms and traditions vary. In Turkmenistan, where well over three-quarters of the people are Sunni Muslims, many worship at the tombs of holy men as well as in mosques.

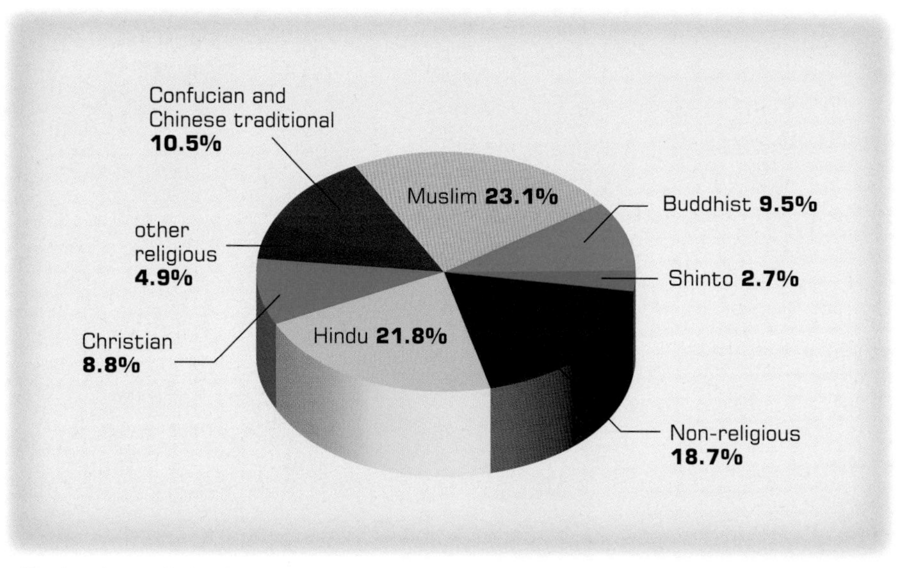

The religious faiths of people in the whole of Asia.

The Potala Palace, in the Tibetan capital Lhasa, was once the residence of the Dalai Lama.

TIBET AND XINJIANG

Tibet (Xizang Zizhiq in Chinese) and Xinjiang are both **autonomous**, or self-governing, regions of China. Their history and culture are very different from the rest of the country, and this is reflected in their religions. Most Tibetans follow Lamaism (also called Tibetan Buddhism), which was introduced there in the 7th century. Until 1959, the head of this religion, the Dalai Lama, was also the ruler of Tibet. After a failed uprising against the ruling Chinese, the Dalai Lama went into exile in India.

Turkic people called Uygurs make up about half of the population of Xinjiang. Many other ethnic groups from Central Asia settled in the region centuries ago, which led to Islam being the major religion there. Like the Buddhist Tibetans, many Muslim Uygurs seek independence from China.

CONFUCIANISM

Confucius is a Latin version of the Chinese title Kongfuzi (meaning "Great Master Kong"), a title given to Kong Qiu (551–479 BCE). Confucius was a teacher of history and poetry, who taught his students to think about the way in which they should live. It is for these teachings that he is still followed, in China and elsewhere, 2,500 years later.

Confucius believed that every person must be truthful, brave, and courteous to others. If families behaved in this way, governments and rulers would be well-ordered too, so a nation's welfare began in ordinary people's homes. When Confucius died, his followers spread his teachings which had a great influence on Chinese government and the lives of ordinary people. Though people call Confucianism a religion, it has no priests and does not teach the worship of gods.

Aiming for educational success

Standards of education vary in the region, but one country stands out for its attitude to educational success – Japan. Free, compulsory education is delivered in primary and middle schools for children aged 6 to 15. Almost all children then continue their education at a three-year high school. There is great competition to get into a good one, because more than two-thirds of students go on to further education, and they want to get into a highly regarded university.

There are more than 500 universities in Japan, and many more hundreds of technical colleges. Two of the most famous are the University of Tokyo, particularly known for its teaching of law and literature, and the University of Kyoto, which has 22,000 students and is famous for science and philosophy. Japanese people think that if you attend a top university you are more likely to get a good job.

Education and the economy

In Asian countries, as elsewhere, governments see a relationship between education – especially the funds spent on education by the state – and the national economy. They expect their educational system to produce young people who are ready and able to help their nation's economy by contributing good work. This is particularly the case in China, where the economy is growing very fast (see page 43). There is still a shortage of schools, however, especially in rural areas. In recent years, the Chinese have worked hard to modernize educational methods to keep up with the economy. Very able students go to "key schools", with the best teachers and equipment. China has more than 2,000 universities and colleges, but there are not enough places for everyone. Adult education is important, and some people continue their education at "workers' colleges", run by companies and factories. There are also many television and Internet courses.

WOMEN IN MONGOLIA

Since 1990, Mongolia has been trying to modernize its economy and educational system. As in many Asian countries, Mongolians used to think that it was not important for girls to be educated. All that has changed. Today there are many more women at university than men: more than three-quarters of the country's graduates are women. Now more than three out of four medical doctors, three out of five lawyers, and seven out of ten teachers are female.

↑ These Uyghur children in Xinjiang, China, have lessons in their own language. About 7 million people speak Uyghur, which is an Altaic language.

Languages

The region's languages come from different language families. More of the world's people speak Chinese than any other language. It has many different **dialects**, and schools teach the Northern form of Chinese known as Mandarin, which is also spoken in Taiwan. Tibetan belongs to the same Sino-Tibetan language family. Japanese and Korean form a language family of their own. The Uralic and Altaic family includes many languages in Central Asia, Mongolia and Siberia. Russian belongs to the Indo-European group of languages.

Main groups of languages

Language family	Language	Country	Speakers in millions worldwide
Sino-Tibetan	Mandarin Chinese	China, Taiwan	873
Indo-European	Russian	Russia	145
Uralic-Altaic	Uzbek	Uzbekistan	18
	Kazakh	Kazakhstan	8
	Turkmen	Turkmenistan	6
	Tajik	Tajikistan	4
	Kyrgyz	Kyrgyzstan	3
	Mongolian	Mongolia	2
Japanese-Korean	Japanese	Japan	122
	Korean	N. Korea, S. Korea	67

88

Culture

Asian arts, customs, and ways of life vary greatly across the **continent**. The region's 12 countries and many more ethnic groups have their own distinctive traditions in artistic fields such as painting and sculpture, architecture and design, music and dance, and drama and literature. Many of these traditions have been handed down from generation to generation over centuries.

East Asia has a particularly old and rich set of artistic traditions, in such fields as architecture, carving, scroll painting, sculpture, and painted **porcelain**. These are inherited from the ancient Chinese Empire, which influenced the whole area, including Japan and Korea. In more recent centuries, Japan has developed its own culture that is known and admired all over the world. North Asia has been most influenced by Russia, which in the 19th century became known worldwide for its drama, literature, classical music, and ballet. Since gaining their independence, the Central Asian republics have largely thrown off the former Russian influence and returned to many of their own individual customs.

← A seven-year-old boy shows his skills in calligraphy at a competition in Tokyo.

↑ Learning *ikebana* is still very popular in Japan. The structure of an arrangement is based on three main points representing heaven, earth, and humankind.

Dramatic performance

The region has many long-standing traditions of stage performance. One of the earliest forms was a kind of opera that began in China in the 14th century. By the mid-19th century, this had developed into *ching-hsi* ("opera of the capital"), or Peking opera, in which songs and dance, along with speech and acrobatics, are performed in colourful costumes. A small orchestra provides the music, and the action is based on Chinese history and folklore. Some of the traditional characters have painted faces. Today, performances are still enjoyed in the capital, Beijing, and in the cities of Tianjin and Shanghai.

One of the most popular forms of traditional Japanese drama is *kabuki* ("song and dance art"), which began in the late 16th century and includes historical plays. It is performed by male actors, who have colourful costumes and make-up and use dramatic gestures and mime to express emotions. This art form is still popular today, and there is a special theatre in Tokyo devoted to performances of *kabuki*.

In the Central Asian countries, traditions of dramatic dance from different cultures were brought along the ancient Silk Road. This was a trade route that led from China, through Central Asia, to Europe. The folk dances of Uzbekistan and neighbouring countries show Chinese, Mongolian, Persian, and Indian influences. Dancers use their hands and arms in an expressive way, circling them around their body and above their head. Sometimes a dancer will kneel on the floor. There are also dramatic spins and turns. Modern Uzbek performers keep the Central Asian traditions alive.

Japanese folds and flowers

Origami (Japanese for "folded paper") is the art of folding paper into decorative shapes and figures. Skilled experts aim to use geometric folds and crease patterns to achieve the desired shape. The figures may be birds (such as a crane), fish, or flowers. The artist starts with a square piece of plain, coloured, or patterned paper, which is not cut or torn. Sometimes foil-backed paper is used.

Ikebana (Japanese for "living flowers") is the traditional art of formal flower arrangement. It began many hundreds of years ago, as a form of ritual offering in Buddhist temples. *Ikebana* is based on simple but important rules, using the harmony of simple linear shapes to bring out the subtle, delicate beauty of the flowers. Compared to showy, decorative arrangements in other parts of the world, the Japanese style is very simple and stylish.

CENTRAL ASIAN EPICS AND SONGS

The tradition of reciting poems and legends about heroic events is kept alive in Kazakhstan and Kyrgyzstan. The most famous Kyrgyz epic is the *Manas*, which tells of great feats by tribal chieftains in the 9th century as they competed and fought with neighbouring tribes. This epic poem is often sung to the accompaniment of a three-stringed instrument called a *komuz*.

Kazakh folk singers also compete with each other in an *aitys*, which includes singers and musicians answering each other's words and tunes as quickly and wittily as possible. The *aitys* keeps alive social and cultural awareness of the Kazakh homeland.

World and regional sports

Major worldwide sports are taken very seriously in this region of Asia. Soccer is popular everywhere, both to play and to watch, and interest in women's soccer is increasing. Russia, Japan, and South Korea have World class teams. Russia also excels at tennis. At the start of the 2007 season, four Russian women were ranked in the world's top 10, with two more in the top 15.

The Olympic Games will be held in Beijing in 2008 (see page 27), and China is keen to show that its athletes are the best in the world. In 2004, China was second in the overall medals table to the USA, which gained just three gold medals more. As the table below shows, Russia, Japan, and South Korea joined China in the top ten medal winners.

In their traditional martial arts, Japan won 8 of the 14 gold medals in judo, and South Korea won most medals in taekwondo. Japan won the bronze medal for baseball. In gymnastics – a popular sport throughout Asia – Japan won the men's team event, and Russia was third in the women's team competition.

← Kazakh falconers hunt on horseback. They wear heavy gloves to protect them from the golden eagles' strong talons. The bird's wingspan is up to 2.2 metres (7 feet).

FALCONRY IN KAZAKHSTAN

The sport of falconry – hunting with trained falcons and other birds of prey – may have begun in ancient China more than 3,000 years ago. In some parts of Central Asia, falconry is still an important sport. In Kazakhstan, birds of prey are still used for hunting as well as for sporting competitions. Falconers use the golden eagle to hunt large prey such as wolves, foxes, and hares.

Medals awarded at the 2004 Olympic Games in Greece

Rank	Country	Gold	Silver	Bronze	Total medals
2	China	32	17	14	63
3	Russia	27	27	38	92
5	Japan	16	9	12	37
9	South Korea	9	12	9	30
31	Taiwan	2	2	1	5
34	Uzbekistan	2	1	2	5
40	Kazakhstan	1	4	3	8
58	North Korea	0	4	1	5
71	Mongolia	0	0	1	1

North Korea's Mass Games

Mass Games are held regularly in North Korea. These are festivals of gymnastics and dance, in which thousands of well-trained, disciplined young people present synchronized routines. Other youngsters use coloured cards to make huge panoramic images as a backdrop to the gymnastics. The Games are held to celebrate the birthday of Kim Il-sung, who was leader of North Korea until 1994. He has the official title of Eternal President, and children are brought up to refer to him as Great Leader.

← Young gymnasts at Mass Games in North Korea. They train hard to be able to participate in the Games.

Chinese New Year

Chinese New Year is probably the most famous of all the region's festivals. It is celebrated by Chinese people all over the world. The date of New Year's Day varies according to the Chinese lunar-solar calendar, so the celebrations can begin any time between 21 January and 20 February. In 2008, the new Chinese Year of the Rat begins on 7 February; in 2009 (Ox) on 26 January; and in 2010 (Tiger) on 14 February.

The full celebration lasts for 15 days. Before New Year's Eve, families traditionally clean their homes to sweep away bad luck. The first week is most important, and much of it is spent celebrating with family and friends. The festivities end with a lantern festival, when children carry lanterns at night and there are lantern parades.

← One of the most popular celebrations at Chinese New Year is the dragon dance.

Mongolian *Naadam*

In Mongolia the national festival is *Naadam*, held on 11–13 July. It is celebrated with archery, horseracing, and wrestling competitions. All three sports are popular throughout Central Asia. This festival is more than 2,000 years old. Traditionally only men took part, but today women archers and riders compete, and there is a special horse race for children. Champions are awarded the titles Elephant, Falcon, Lion, and Titan.

Japanese people eat a huge amount of fish. One traditional way of eating it is as *sushi*, raw with rice, egg, or vegetables. This modern sushi bar is in Tokyo.

Asian food

In a myth of ancient China, the Chinese man – Han – differs from the rest of the world's "savages" in two important ways: he eats cereals and he uses fire to cook his food. Today, cereals are still staples in the Chinese diet, with rice or noodles being served with main meals. In northern China, the noodles are made from wheat-flour, in the south from rice. The food is stir-fried in a wok (a metal pan with a curved base), and may include pieces of meat, fish, and vegetables. It is eaten with chopsticks.

In Russia and Central Asia, traditional dishes have also been handed down over the centuries. Some well-known Russian examples are *kasha* (porridge made with buckwheat), and *piroshki* (savoury pastries filled with meat or fish and rice). In Siberia, people eat dairy products and vegetables in summer, and meat dishes with pickled vegetables in winter. One popular Siberian dish is *pelmeni* (small dumplings with a meat filling).

J-POP, *ANIME* AND *MANGA*

Japan has a strong popular culture based on music and films. J-pop (or Japanese pop) developed from American and European music, which inspired young Japanese musicians to create their own pop scene. Television talent shows have also launched successful boy and girl bands. The arts of *anime* (Japanese animation) and *manga* (cartoons and comic books) have had an impact around the world. Many have science-fiction or fantasy themes.

Natural resources and economy

This Asian region is rich in natural resources, including coal, oil, natural gas, forests, and rivers. The use of these energy sources for industrialization developed later than in Europe or North America, but much of the region has now caught up with the rest of the world. Japan expanded its economy during the second half of the 20th century, and in the past decade China (which has more than ten times as many people) has been doing the same.

Today, Japan has the world's second-largest economy (after the USA) and China comes in fourth (after Germany). China's economy has been growing at an incredible rate of nearly 10 percent a year. Some experts predict that it will be the world's strongest economy by 2020. The region's other strong economies are South Korea, Russia, and Taiwan.

Kazakhstan has the largest economy in Central Asia. Agriculture makes up more than half of its economic production, with livestock and grain being very important. Another third is produced by industry, especially mining and oil and gas production. Russia is one of the country's most important trading partners. The Russians continue to launch their spacecraft from a leased site in Kazakhstan, as they did in the days of the former Soviet Union.

← South Korean workers stand in formation at the launch of a ship at the port of Ulsan. This is the world's largest shipyard (see page 51).

Energy sources

The region relies on **fossil fuels** (coal, oil, and natural gas) to provide most of its energy. China is by far the world's biggest producer of coal: its provides 45 percent of the world total, producing more than twice as much as it did 20 years ago. Russia and Kazakhstan are also large coal producers. China exports only a very small percentage of its coal, so is also the world's biggest coal consumer. Japan's coal industry, on the other hand, has declined and the country imports most of its coal.

Russia is the world's leading producer of natural gas. Many other countries import gas from Russia, some through long pipelines. Uzbekistan and Turkmenistan each produce about a tenth as much gas as Russia. Russia is also the world's second biggest producer of oil, after Saudi Arabia; China and Kazakhstan are also large oil producers. However, China and Japan both import a lot of oil, and China is the world's second biggest oil consumer, after the USA. Because of this, China will put the world's energy resources under great pressure as its economy continues to grow. All fossil fuels are non-renewable – they cannot be replaced and will one day run out – so many countries are looking to increase their use of renewable sources of energy. The table opposite shows the energy sources in the region's top four economies, plus Uzbekistan for comparison. The largest energy source for each country appears in **bold**.

← The wall of the Three Gorges Dam, completed in 2006, is 2,309 metres (7,576 feet) long and 185 metres (607 feet) high. Power generated here will be sent to eastern and central China, bringing electricity to some villages for the first time.

Percentage of energy sources used to produce electricity in the region

	Coal %	Oil %	Gas %	Nuclear %	Renewables %
China	**79.4**	3.0	0.3	2.3	15.0
Japan	**28.2**	13.2	24.3	23.1	11.2
Russia	18.8	3.0	**44.5**	16.4	17.3
South Korea	**38.9**	9.2	12.3	37.6	2.0
Uzbekistan	2.9	11.4	**72.9**	0.0	12.8

Hydroelectric power

Hydroelectric (or water) power from river dams is the greatest contributor to the renewables column in the table above. There are also large electricity-producing dams in Kyrgyzstan and Tajikistan. The most powerful hydroelectric plant in the world is being built in China. When it is completed in 2009, the Three Gorges Dam on the Chang Jiang river will produce 18,200 megawatts of electricity from its 26 generators. That is nearly three times as much as the biggest hydroelectric dam in Russia, on the Yenisei River.

THE NUCLEAR OPTION

More than a third of South Korea's electricity (and nearly a quarter of Japan's) is produced by nuclear power stations. These percentages may increase, and by 2010 the two countries will have 97 nuclear plants. There is opposition to nuclear power because of the risk of accidents and the great problem of how to dispose safely of radioactive waste. In 1995 there was a leak of coolant at the Monju fast-breeder reactor in Japan. No one was injured, but the plant has remained shut down ever since.

Agriculture

The main crop-growing areas of the region are in East Asia (China) and southwestern North Asia (Russia). Most of Central Asia is too dry, and much of North Asia is too cold, to be suitable for agriculture. Central and eastern China are very good farming areas, where agriculture has been practised for thousands of years. In recent years, China has come to dominate production of many of the world's crops, including two of the most important cereals – rice and wheat (see table on page 46). Russia is the largest producer of barley, oats, and rye.

Crops in which China leads the world in production

Cereals	Vegetables	Fruits and nuts	Others
buckwheat	asparagus	apples	hens' eggs
rice	cabbages	chestnuts	honey
wheat	carrots	melons	sheep's milk
	cauliflower	peaches	tea
	cucumbers	pears	
	garlic	plums	
	green beans	sesame seeds	
	green chillies and peppers	tomatoes	
	lettuce	walnuts	
	mushrooms		
	potatoes		
	pumpkins		
	spinach		

This map shows the cropland, grazing land, and forest land across the region.

Nomadic herders look after their goats on the grasslands of Mongolia.

MONGOLIAN HERDERS

Mongolia's agriculture, which forms a major part of its economy, is based mainly on livestock – sheep, goats, cattle, horses, and camels. There are many large farms, but a few Mongolian families still live their traditional **nomadic** life, moving with their animals to find pasture land, especially in the wetter north-central areas of the country. Nomads live in round felt tents called yurts, which provide protection from the cold and can be taken down and moved on when necessary.

Cotton production

China is the world's largest producer of cotton. Uzbekistan is also a large producer. Cotton is very important to the Uzbek economy, but there are problems to be solved. As described on page 19, the **irrigation** of dry land for cotton-growing is shrinking the Aral Sea. Much of Uzbekistan's agriculture is manual rather than mechanical and, according to the Environmental Justice Foundation, child labour is used for cotton-picking. This group is calling on the European Union and others to stop importing Uzbek cotton until this practice is stopped.

Fishing and aquaculture

Fishing is very important all along the Pacific coastline, and China catches more fish than any other country in the world (about a third of world production). Japan is the fifth largest fishing country (after Peru, the USA and Indonesia). Both nations are also strong in **aquaculture**, or fish farming, which is a growing industry and makes up a quarter of global fisheries production. China specializes in farming carp, while Japan specializes in amberjack, scallops, and oysters.

Manufacturing industry

There is a great deal of heavy industry in China, Japan, North Korea, South Korea, and Taiwan. Large factories produce steel and goods such as cars and other road vehicles, electronic equipment, and ships (see page 51). The region produces more than half the world's steel (see bar chart below). In China, steel production tripled between 2001 and 2006, and China also became the world's biggest exporter of steel.

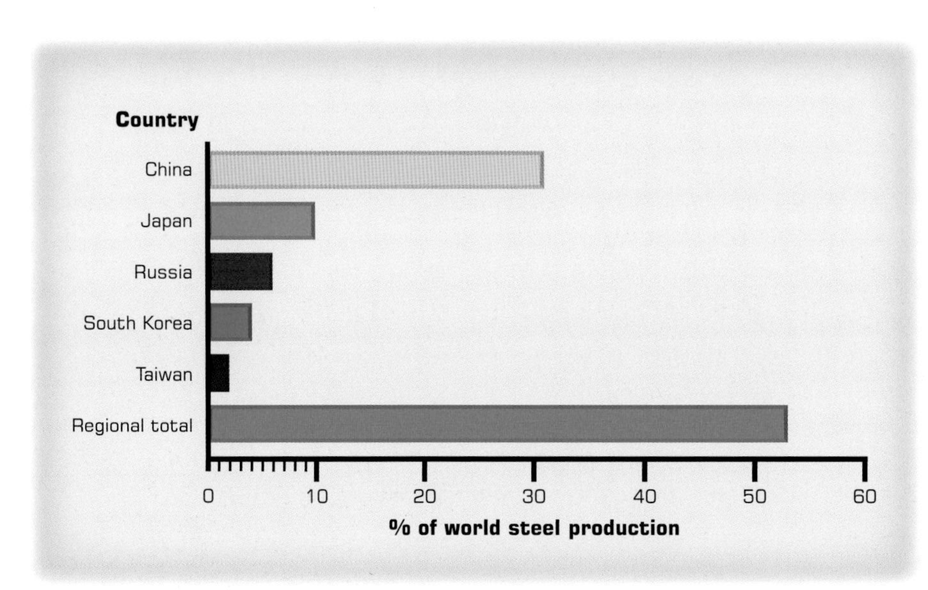

This bar chart shows the percentage of world steel production in five of the region's countries.

We know little about the economy of North Korea, because its government does not issue official figures. Experts believe that iron ore is mined there, as well as coal, graphite, lead, zinc, and precious metals. State-owned factories produce steel, chemicals, machinery, textiles, and weapons.

Japanese cars

Japan is the world's biggest producer of cars, producing more than 9 million in 2005. Including overseas production, more than 6 million of those cars were made by Toyota, with Nissan and Honda the next biggest companies. The car industry in South Korea has grown by 30 percent over the past five years. The largest manufacturer there is Hyundai.

Passenger cars produced in 2005

Country	Cars in millions	% world production
Japan	9.1	19.8
South Korea	3.4	7.4
China	3.1	6.7
Russia	1.1	2.4
Taiwan	0.3	0.7
Uzbekistan	0.09	0.2
Regional total	17.1	37.2
World total	46.0	

SOUTH KOREAN CONGLOMERATES

Since 1961, when government policy changed, South Korean industry has been dominated by a number of large family-controlled **conglomerates**, called *chaebol* (or *jaebeol*), meaning "business associations". The government and big banks helped finance these companies, which grew rapidly into the 1990s. In 1997 there was an economic crisis in East Asia, which put an end to some of the *chaebol*. One of their greatest problems was that they had enormous export markets but only a small domestic market (48 million South Koreans), and that there were too many large companies competing with each other.

Some *chaebol* survived the crisis and have continued to grow. The largest company is Samsung, founded in 1938 and best known for its electronic products – mobile phones, televisions and audio players, and home appliances such as refrigerators and microwave ovens. Next largest is car manufacturer Hyundai, founded in 1946, which also has factories in China, India, and North America. Then comes the LG group (formerly known as Lucky Goldstar), founded in 1947, which manufactures electronic goods, chemicals, and telecommunications.

↑ Many East Asian companies specialize in producing electronic equipment and other high-tech goods. This modern factory in South Korea makes plasma display panels (PDPs).

Economy and wealth

A country's economy includes its production and consumption of goods and services. The economic performance of the region's countries varies enormously, and national economies are not growing at an even rate across the **continent**. The richer industrial countries – such as Japan, China, and South Korea – continue to gain wealth at a faster rate than poorer countries, such as Kyrgyzstan, Tajikistan, and Mongolia.

Figures showing **gross domestic product** (GDP) indicate how the economic performance of a country compares with that of others. GDP is the total value of all a country's goods and services (not including any extra income from investment in other countries). In the following chart, GDP has been divided by population to give an amount per person, so that the wealth of different countries' citizens can be compared easily. The chart shows how the region's 12 countries vary. The average GDP per person is 26 times higher in Japan than in Tajikistan. Chinese people will hope to increase their wealth in the coming years, as their economy continues to grow.

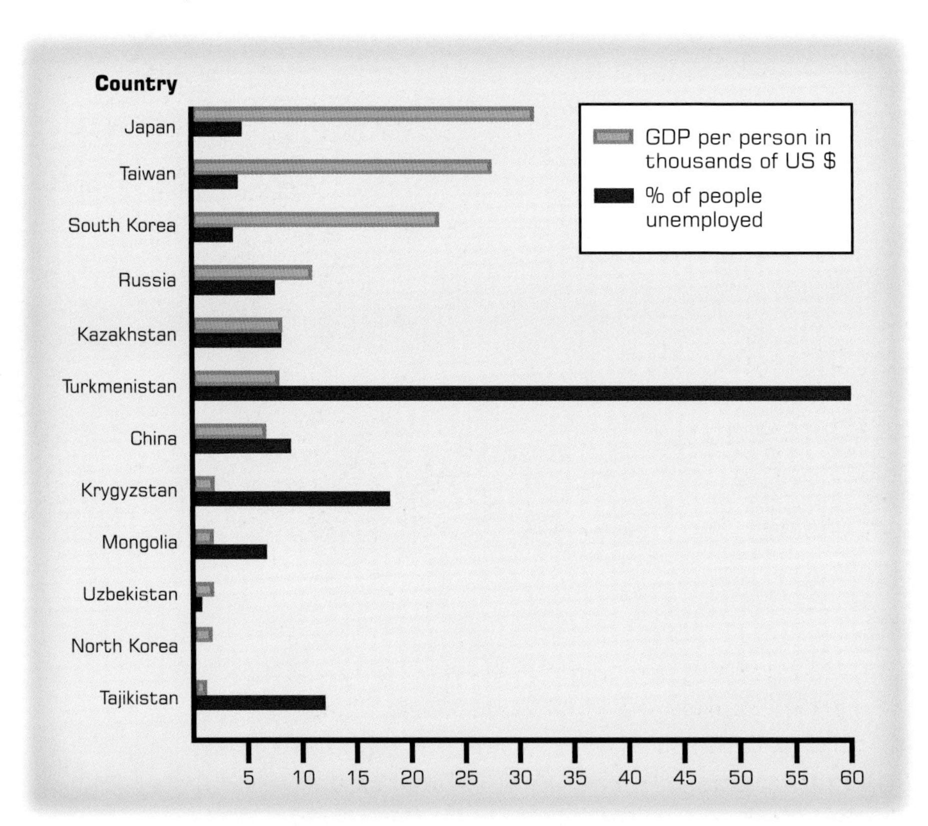

The figures show that unemployment rates vary across the region, as they do around the world. The figure for Turkmenistan is disastrous. No figures are available for North Korea, and its GDP is an estimate.

TURKMENISTAN

Turkmenistan has not benefited fully from its gas and oil resources. This is partly because of disputes with other states bordering the Caspian Sea over how the area's oil is divided up. There has also been a disagreement over prices with Russia, which buys about two-thirds of Turkmenistan's natural gas. According to the United Nations Children's Fund, the country's economic problems particularly affect its young people:

> Only 55 percent of the population has access to safe drinking water (24 percent in rural areas). The government has announced a goal of 100 percent access to safe drinking water by 2020.

Because teenagers are expected to help with agricultural work, the school year is only 150 days long and the curriculum does not adequately cover the core subjects.

Enrolment in universities has declined from 40,000 in the 1990s to 3,000 in 2004. Students must work for two years before attending college, and this is difficult for them to achieve given Turkmenistan's high unemployment rate.

The president has publicly asked local governors to stop the use of child labour in picking cotton (see page 47).

← These pipelines carry oil from Turkmenistan to the refinery.

Shipbuilding

East Asia dominates the world's shipbuilding, with the following shares of the global market: South Korea 37.3%, Japan 24%, China 17%, Taiwan 1.4%. The busiest shipyards in the world are in southeast South Korea, at the industrial port of Ulsan. Before 1962, when it was developed, this was a fishing port. Then major industries moved to the area, including an oil refinery and a car plant, and the nearby shipbuilding port of Pangojin became part of the growing city.

Growth of China

Since 1978, China's gross domestic product has increased more than tenfold. The Chinese economy has been growing by about 9 percent a year in recent times, and this trend is expected to continue. Nevertheless, millions of people who live in the countryside have been left behind by this growth. The overall GDP per person is still less than a quarter that of Japanese people, and it has been estimated that 150 million Chinese live below the poverty line.

Another problem in China is pollution. Worsening air quality, soil erosion and a lack of clean water resources are of great concern to **environmentalists**. Much farmland is being lost because of poor soil and industrial development. All the world's industrial countries are facing these problems. The Chinese government has stated that protection of the environment and conservation of resources are basic goals.

The Great Wall is one of the most popular attractions for visitors to China. It was begun more than 2,000 years ago, as a defence against northern invaders. Eventually the 9-metre (29-foot) high wall stretched for about 2,700 kilometres (1,680 miles) across the Chinese Empire.

At the same time as the growth in its economy, China has seen a huge increase in tourism. In 1980, when China was still seen as not very welcoming to outsiders, the country earned US$ 600 million from international tourism. By 2005, this figure had increased to more than US$ 29,000 million. According to the China National Tourism Administration, this was achieved by welcoming 120 million tourists – more than twice the number who visited just 10 years previously.

East Asian Tigers

During the late 20th century, Hong Kong (seen as separate economically from China), South Korea, and Taiwan – along with Singapore, on the southern tip of the Malaysian **peninsula** – came to be called the East Asian Tigers. The name referred to their "tiger" economies, meaning they were very dynamic and growing fast. All were led by exports, rather than their home markets. Since a highly skilled workforce was required to manufacture goods, standards of education were considered important by all the Tigers. However, labour had to remain cheap so that prices were competitive, so the workers were not paid particularly well.

In 1997 there was a financial crisis in East Asia, which put great pressure on the Tiger economies. Many people came to realize that a strong home market is as important as export success. After a difficult period, the Tigers have become stable again, though perhaps less "tigerish".

HONG KONG AND MACAO

Hong Kong is a former British **dependency** on the southern coast of China. It was returned by the UK to China in 1997, and China declared it a special administrative region (SAR). The Chinese government agreed that Hong Kong would be allowed to keep its free enterprise, capitalist economy within the overall communist system.

There was a similar situation in Macao, further down the coast, which used to be a colony of Portugal. It was returned to China in 1999. Both SARs are run by China under an arrangement known as "one country, two systems". China has offered the same arrangement to Taiwan, but this has been refused.

Transport

China has the greatest number of roads in the region. Japan, although 25 times smaller than China, has two-thirds as many roads. Japan also has a high rate of private car ownership (431 cars per 1,000 people), while Russia has 157 per 1,000, and China just 11 per 1,000. However, car ownership is growing fast in China.

Transport networks

	railways in km (miles)	roads in millions of km (miles)	waterways in km (miles)
Russia	87,157 (54,168)	0.9 (0.6)	102,000 (63,393)
China	74,408 (46,245)	1.8 (1.1)	123,964 (77,044)
Japan	23,556 (14,640)	1.2 (0.8)	1,770 (1,100)
Kazakhstan	13,700 (8,515)	0.3 (0.2)	4,000 (2,486)
North Korea	5,214 (3,241)	0.03 (0.02)	2,250 (1,398)

Japan has invested heavily in its railway system. An electric high-speed railway between Tokyo and Osaka opened as early as 1964, and the network has since grown across Japan. Today almost half of Japan's railways are electrified. The Shinkansen super express trains are so fast that they are known as "bullet trains". Since 1970, a maglev (magnetic levitation) train has also been in development. This floats on a magnetic field and is driven along a guideway by magnets. In 2003, a Shinkansen maglev train reached a world-record speed of 581 kph (361 mph).

← A train crosses the La Sa Te bridge near Lhasa. The city lies at a height of 3,650 metres (11,975 feet).

PAN-HIMALAYAN RAILWAY

In 2006, a railway line was completed between Golmud, in the Qinghai province of China, and Lhasa in Tibet. This final section of the longer Qingzang railway is 1,142 kilometres (710 miles) long and took four years to build. Trains climb up to the Tibetan Plateau, making this the highest railway in the world. The carriages are sealed, to protect passengers from altitude sickness.

The longest single railway in the region is in Russia. The Trans-Siberian Railway, which runs from Moscow in European Russia to Vladivostok on the Pacific coast, first opened in 1916. It took 14 years to lay more than 9,000 kilometres (5,590 miles) of track. A branch line runs south from Ulan-Ude to the east of Lake Baikal. This Trans-Mongolian express heads south through Mongolia to Beijing, linking the capitals of Russia (Moscow), Mongolia (Ulan Bator) and China (Beijing). The whole line has become a tourist attraction for international travellers.

Transport networks in the Central Asian countries are poor. This is holding countries back in their efforts to develop their economies and reduce poverty. Governments are trying to overcome this problem by developing public transport systems.

Flying in and out

East Asia has some of the world's biggest, busiest airports. More than 200 million passengers use the top five every year, and this number is increasing. The International Air Transport Association forecasts that the amount of passenger air traffic to and from China will grow by 10 percent in 2005–2009. Freight traffic will grow even more, by nearly 15 percent, the biggest forecast increase of any country in the world.

Japan has two of the busiest airports in Asia - Haneda (Tokyo) and Narita (near Tokyo) - and in 1994 a new airport opened near Osaka. This one is a bit different because it is an offshore airport, built on a specially made artificial island 5 kilometres (3.1 miles) off the coast. The airport can stay open 24 hours a day, as planes take off and land over the sea and do not disturb people. The island is connected to the mainland by a double-decker rail and road bridge. So far the airport has survived a major earthquake and a **typhoon**.

Fact file

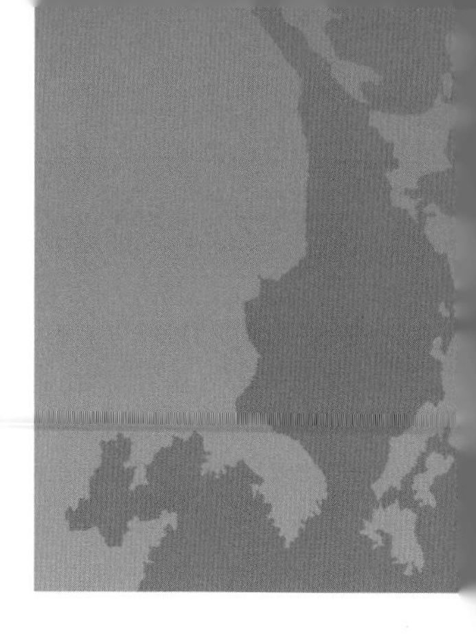

Independent countries of North and East Asia

Name	Area in sq km (sq miles)	Population	Capital
China	9,563,980 (3,692,674)	1,346,606,000	Beijing
Japan	377,873 (145,898)	127,994,000	Tokyo
Kazakhstan	2,604,200 (1,005,487)	14,906,000	Astana
Kyrgyzstan	199,000 (76,834)	5,336,000	Bishkek
Mongolia	1,564,116 (603,909)	2,670,000	Ulan Bator
North Korea	120,538 (46,540)	23,059,000	Pyongyang
Russia (Asian)	12,788,842 (4,937,800)	36,753,000	Moscow
South Korea	99,538 (38,432)	48,877,000	Seoul
Taiwan*	36,006 (13,902)	23,111,000	Taipei
Tajikistan	142,100 (54,865)	7,292,000	Dushanbe
Turkmenistan	488,100 (188,456)	5,232,000	Ashgabat
Uzbekistan	447,400 (172,742)	27,890,000	Tashkent

*It is disputed whether Taiwan is an independent country; see page 28

Timeline

c. 7000 BCE	Rice is being cultivated in China.
c. 2700 BCE	Silk is discovered in China.
1766 BCE	The traditional date of the beginning of the Shang **dynasty** in China.
c. 1600 BCE	The start of the Bronze Age in China.
c. 660 BCE	Jimmu, legendary first emperor of Japan, comes to power.
c. 650 BCE	Iron technology is being used in China; the first sections are built that later become the Great Wall of China.
551–479 BCE	The life of Confucius.
221 BCE	Qin ruler Shi Huangdi unites China as the first emperor.
202 BCE–9 CE	The Han dynasty rules China.
c. 112 BCE	The Silk Road opens across Asia, from China to Europe.
57 CE	Japanese messengers travel to China.
166	Roman merchants visit the Chinese imperial court.
317	Huns from Mongolia conquer northern China.
607–842	The Tibetan Empire is unified.
668	Korea is unified under Silla.
745–840	The Uyghur Empire flourishes in Mongolia.
1185	The first shogunate is founded in Japan.
1206	Mongols under Genghis Khan begin the conquest of Asia.

1264	Kublai Khan founds the Mongol Yuan dynasty in China.
1274–81	Mongol attacks on Japan are defeated.
1275–92	Venetian traveller Marco Polo visits China.
1368–1644	The Ming dynasty rules China.
1370–1405	Mongol conqueror Timur rules his empire from Samarkand (Uzbekistan).
1543	Portuguese traders arrive in Japan.
1557	A Portuguese enclave is founded at Macao.
1603–1867	Rule of the Tokugawa shogunate in Japan.
1697	The Chinese occupy "Outer" Mongolia.
1751	China overruns Tibet.
1830–54	The Russian conquest of Kazakhstan.
1839–42	The First Opium War between Britain and China; Britain annexes Hong Kong.
1894–95	The Russo-Japanese War; Japan occupies Formosa (Taiwan).
1905	Japan defeats Russia and takes control in Korea and Manchuria.
1911	The Chinese Revolution overthrows the emperor.
1916	The Trans Siberian Railway is completed.
1917	The Russian Revolution overthrows the monarchy and establishes a **communist** state.
1922–91	The period of the Soviet Union, made up of 15 communist **republics** including Russia and five Central Asian states.
1937–38	Japan occupies central China.
1941–45	Japan fights the Allied Powers in the Pacific during World War II; in 1945 the USA drops atomic bombs on Hiroshima and Nagasaki in Japan, forcing a Japanese surrender.
1949	Chinese communists conquer mainland China; Mao Zedong (1893–1976) sets up the People's Republic; nationalists under Chiang Kai-shek retreat to Taiwan.
1950	China invades Tibet.

1950–53	The Korean War.
1951	The USA ends the occupation of Japan.
1966–69	Mao Zedong introduces a Cultural Revolution in China.
1991	The Soviet Union breaks up into separate republics.
1997	Control of Hong Kong returns to China from the UK.
1999	Control of Macao returns to China from Portugal.
2000	The leaders of North and South Korea meet for the first time since Korea was divided.
2005	Turkmenistan downgrades its CIS status to associate member.

Glossary

aquaculture	fish farming
autonomous	self-governing
capitalism	political system based on the private ownership of property and wealth, with free, competitive markets
charter	formal statement describing rights and responsibilities
climate	general weather conditions in an area over a long period of time
Cold War	state of political hostility between the Soviet bloc and the western countries (1946–91)
communism	political system based on the communal ownership of property and wealth, with regulated markets
conglomerate	large business organization
coniferous	referring to conifers, cone-bearing trees with needle-like leaves
continent	one of the Earth's seven huge land masses
dependency	territory controlled by another country
dialect	regional variety of a language
dynasty	series of rulers from the same family
environmentalist	person who is concerned about and acts to protect the natural environment
fossil fuel	fuel (such as coal, oil, and natural gas) that comes from the fossilized remains of prehistoric plants and animals
geologist	scientist who studies the structure of the Earth
glacier	large mass of ice that fills a valley and moves very slowly down it
global warming	the heating up of the Earth's surface, especially caused by pollution from burning fossil fuels
gorge	deep and narrow valley

greenhouse gas gas such as carbon dioxide that traps the Sun's heat and increases the greenhouse effect

gross domestic product the total value of all a country's goods and services, not including any extra income from investment in other countries

headwaters streams that form the beginning of a river

hydroelectricity electricity produced by moving water, especially from a dam across a river

irrigate to water land in order to help crops to grow

monsoon large-scale seasonal wind

nomadic referring to a group of people (nomads) who constantly move from place to place in search of pasture for their animals

peninsula piece of land that juts out into the sea

permafrost permanently frozen subsoil

pilgrim person who goes on a journey to a holy place

plateau flat area of high land

population density the number of people who live in a standard area (such as a square kilometre or a square mile)

porcelain fine white china

precipitation rain, snow, sleet, or hail

republic state in which power is held by the people and their elected representatives, with a president rather than a monarch

Ring of Fire zone around the Pacific Ocean, where there are many active volcanoes and earthquakes are common

silt fine mud and clay carried and deposited by rivers

strait narrow passage of water connecting two seas

subarctic referring to the region just south of the Arctic Circle

subcontinent large region that forms a separate part of a continent

taiga northern coniferous forest immediately south of the tundra

time zone one of the areas into which the world is divided where the same standard time is used

tributary smaller branch of a larger river

tundra flat treeless Arctic region that has permanently frozen subsoil

typhoon violent tropical storm

Find out more

Further reading

Continents of the World: Asia, Rob Bowden (Wayland, 2005)
Central Asia, Paul Clammer (Lonely Planet, 2004)
China, Damian Harper (Lonely Planet, 2005)
Japan, Chris Rowthorn (Lonely Planet, 2005)
In Siberia, Colin Thubron (Penguin, 2000)

Websites

www.unescap.org
The United Nations Economic and Social Commission for Asia and the Pacific (UNESCAP) analyzes social and economic trends across the Asian region.

www.lonelyplanet.com/worldguide/destinations/asia
Travel guide to individual Asian countries, with "fast facts", featured attractions, and tourist information.

news.bbc.co.uk/1/hi/in_depth/asia_pacific/2005/central_asia
"Inside Central Asia", the BBC's in-depth guide to the region, including reports, analysis, maps, facts, figures, and profiles of the five countries.

www.lib.berkeley.edu/EAL
The East Asian Library of the University of California has links to information on China, Japan, and Korea.

old.cnta.gov.cn/lyen/index.asp
China National Tourism Administration, website "directly regulated by the state council", with facts and figures, travel tips, and general information on the People's Republic of China.

www.gio.gov.tw
Official information on the Republic of China (Taiwan), including its bid to join the United Nations.

www.unccd.int
The United Nations Convention to Combat Desertification has challenging information on how best to stop deserts growing, including those in Central Asia, Mongolia, and northern China.

news.bbc.co.uk/1/hi/world/asia-pacific/678898.stm
A BBC case study on the shrinking Aral Sea, as part of a series on the world water crisis; the site includes links for further study.

Activities

Here are some topics to research if you want to find out more about the region:

An Asian Union
Would it be a good idea for Asian nations to form an economic and political union (rather like the European Union)? Do North, Central, and East Asians want this? You could start by reading a positive approach by the Japanese Toda Institute, a Buddhist organization, at www.toda.org/Default.aspx?PageID=152

Environmental issues in China
How can the Chinese environment cope with the country's rapid economic expansion? For starting points, see *China's Environmental Challenge: the way forward*, an online publication of the Ecological Society of America, a non-profit scientific organization founded in 1915; subjects include rapid urban expansion, air pollution, and water problems: www.frontiersinecology.org/specialissueChina.php

Independence for Tibet
Should Tibet be granted independence by China? Would it be able to survive on its own? Tibet Online presents the Tibetan side of the debate; it states that the site is dedicated to His Holiness the 14th Dalai Lama, "the heart and soul of the Tibetan nation". Look at www.tibet.orgwith facts and figures, travel tips, and general information on the People's Republic of China.

Index